Taylor Swift

FOR CLARINET

ISBN 978-1-70519-267-2

Visit Hal Leonard Online at
www.halleonard.com

World headquarters, contact:
Hal Leonard
7777 West Bluemound Road
Milwaukee, WI 53213
Email: info@halleonard.com

In Europe, contact:
Hal Leonard Europe Limited
1 Red Place
London, W1K 6PL
Email: info@halleonardeurope.com

In Australia, contact:
Hal Leonard Australia Pty. Ltd.
4 Lentara Court
Cheltenham, Victoria, 3192 Australia
Email: info@halleonard.com.au

ALL TOO WELL

CLARINET

Words and Music by TAYLOR SWIFT
and LIZ ROSE

ANTI-HERO

CLARINET

Words and Music by TAYLOR SWIFT
and JACK ANTONOFF

CHANGE

CLARINET

Words and Music by
TAYLOR SWIFT

BACK TO DECEMBER

CLARINET

Words and Music by
TAYLOR SWIFT

D.S. al Coda

CODA

BLANK SPACE

CLARINET

Words and Music by TAYLOR SWIFT,
MAX MARTIN and SHELLBACK

CARDIGAN

CLARINET

Words and Music by TAYLOR SWIFT
and AARON DESSNER

CHAMPAGNE PROBLEMS

CLARINET

Words and Music by TAYLOR SWIFT
and WILLIAM BOWERY

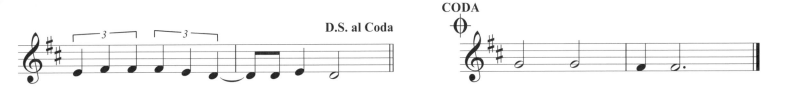

EVERMORE

CLARINET

Words and Music by TAYLOR SWIFT,
WILLIAM BOWERY and JUSTIN VERNON

Tempo I

D.S. al Coda

rit.

CODA

EXILE

CLARINET

Words and Music by TAYLOR SWIFT,
WILLIAM BOWERY and JUSTIN VERNON

To Coda

D.S. al Coda

CODA

FEARLESS

CLARINET

Words and Music by TAYLOR SWIFT,
LIZ ROSE and HILLARY LINDSEY

FIFTEEN

CLARINET

Words and Music by
TAYLOR SWIFT

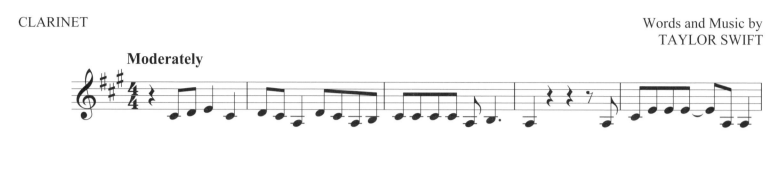

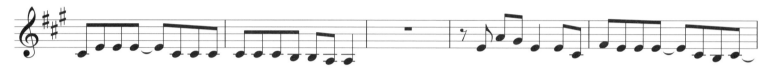

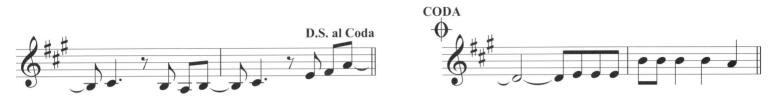

D.S. al Coda

CODA

I KNEW YOU WERE TROUBLE

CLARINET

Words and Music by TAYLOR SWIFT,
SHELLBACK and MAX MARTIN

LAVENDER HAZE

Clarinet

Words and Music by TAYLOR SWIFT,
ZOË KRAVITZ, JACK ANTONOFF,
MARK ANTHONY SPEARS,
SAM DEW and JAHAAN AKIL SWEET

LOVE STORY

CLARINET

Words and Music by
TAYLOR SWIFT

MEAN

CLARINET

Words and Music by
TAYLOR SWIFT

MINE

CLARINET

Words and Music by
TAYLOR SWIFT

Moderately fast

THE 1

CLARINET

Words and Music by TAYLOR SWIFT
and AARON DESSNER

D.S. al Coda
(with repeat)

CODA

OUR SONG

CLARINET

Words and Music by
TAYLOR SWIFT

rit.

PICTURE TO BURN

CLARINET

Words and Music by TAYLOR SWIFT
and LIZ ROSE

SHAKE IT OFF

CLARINET

Words and Music by TAYLOR SWIFT,
MAX MARTIN and SHELLBACK

CODA

SHOULD'VE SAID NO

CLARINET

Words and Music by
TAYLOR SWIFT

SPARKS FLY

CLARINET

Words and Music by
TAYLOR SWIFT

D.S. al Coda

CODA

SPEAK NOW

CLARINET

Words and Music by
TAYLOR SWIFT

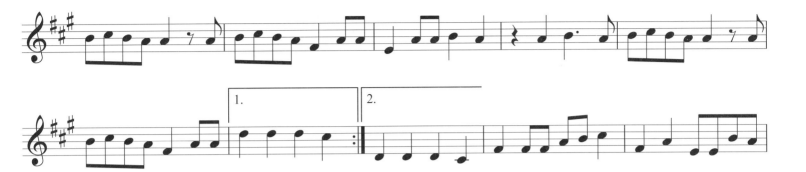

SWEET NOTHING

Clarinet

Words and Music by TAYLOR SWIFT
and WILLAM BOWERY

Simply, in 2

D.S. al Coda

CODA

TEARDROPS ON MY GUITAR

Clarinet

Words and Music by TAYLOR SWIFT
and LIZ ROSE

TODAY WAS A FAIRYTALE

CLARINET

Words and Music by
TAYLOR SWIFT

D.S. al Coda

CODA

1.

2.

22

CLARINET

Words and Music by TAYLOR SWIFT,
SHELLBACK and MAX MARTIN

Moderately

WE ARE NEVER EVER GETTING BACK TOGETHER

CLARINET

Words and Music by TAYLOR SWIFT,
MAX MARTIN and SHELLBACK

WHITE HORSE

CLARINET

Words and Music by TAYLOR SWIFT
and LIZ ROSE

Moderately

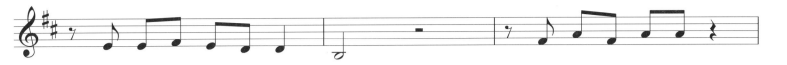

rit.

WILLOW

CLARINET

Words and Music by TAYLOR SWIFT
and AARON DESSNER

YOU BELONG WITH ME

CLARINET

Words and Music by TAYLOR SWIFT
and LIZ ROSE

D.S. al Coda

CODA

1.

2.

YOU NEED TO CALM DOWN

Clarinet

Words and Music by TAYLOR SWIFT
and JOEL LITTLE

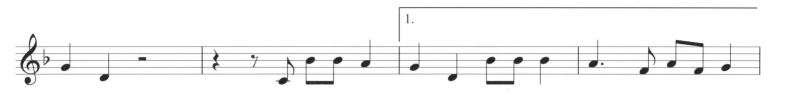

LOOK WHAT YOU MADE ME DO

Clarinet

Words and Music by TAYLOR SWIFT,
JACK ANTONOFF, RICHARD FAIRBRASS,
FRED FAIRBRASS and ROB MANZOLI